Bradwell's Bo

Kent

a Feast of **Fun, Facts** and **History!**

Published by Bradwell Books
9 Orgreave Close Sheffield S13 9NP
Email: books@bradwellbooks.co.uk

British Library Cataloguing in Publication Data: a catalogue record for this book is available from the British Library.

1st Edition

ISBN: 9781909914711

Design & Typesetting by: Andrew Caffrey

Print: Gutenberg Press, Malta

Photograph Credits: Shutterstock, iStock, Creative Commons and credited individually. All other images are by the author.

Mapping: Ordnance Survey Mapping used under licence from the Ordnance Survey.

Ordnance Survey Partner Number 100039353

BIBLIOGRAPHY

A Dictionary of Kentish Dialect by W.D. PARISH and W.F. SHAW (first published 1888)

The Traditional Games of England, Scotland, and Ireland With Tunes by ALICE BERTHA GOMME (Nabu Press 2013)

Percy Maylam's The Kent Hooden Horse by RICHARD MAYLAM and GEOFF DOEL (2009)

Kent Murders by LINDA STRATMANN (Sutton True Crime History) (2009)

Kent Murder Casebook: Sensational Crimes that Shook the County by W. H. JOHNSON (Mystery & Murder 1998)

A Dreadful Murder by MINETTE WALTERS (2013) (the fictionalised story of Caroline Luard's death)

Doctor Syn: A Smuggler Tale of Romney Marsh by RUSSELL THORNDIKE (first published in 1915)

USEFUL WEBSITES

www.visitkent.co.uk

www.historic-kent.co.uk

www.hauntedrooms.co.uk

www.hauntedkent.net

ACKNOWLEDGEMENTS

The Rochester Walk is loosely based on A Dickens of a Walk at Rochester, The AA Walks, AA Media Limited (2013), with additional research.

Engraving of Anne Boleyn: digital restoration by Steven Wynn Photography

Lees Court, Sheldwich image from the British Library Kentish Pudding Pie Photo from Kate's Puddings blogspot

Bradwell's Book of

Kent

a Feast of Fun, Facts and History!

ARDELLA JONES

BRADWELL
BOOKS

Contents

WALKS

Kent has some wonderful walks for all ages and abilities. We've chosen two for you: one round historic Rochester for lovers of Dickens and castles; the other is a circular walk around Margate exploring this flourishing seaside town.

LOCAL CUSTOMS

Kent boasts many modern festivals celebrating its rich history as well as ancient pagan traditions revived to keep old customs alive and kicking.

LOCAL HISTORY

Kent's historic towns and ancient castles tell the history of England from the Roman invasion and the Norman Conquest to Nelson's navy and the Battle of Britain. You can visit Darwin's home at Downe or Churchill's house at Chartwell.

GHOST STORIES

Kent's rustic pubs, timbered cottages and ancient castles conceal a nocturnal world of spirits and spectres with stories to tell. You can even join an after dark ghost tour or book a room in a haunted inn.

LOCAL SPORTS

There's more to Kentish sport than cricket, and the village green and the local pub provide perfect places for traditional games and sports.

FAMOUS LOCALS

Kent boasts so many famous sons and daughters, it was hard to choose just a few from the arts, politics and sport.

Introduction

One and a half million people live in Kent and many more enjoy visiting this fascinating region of south-east England

Kent is a county of contrasts, stretching from the sandy beaches of Ramsgate, through the picturesque hamlets of the Weald, to suburban Dartford, a traditional gateway to London. Kent has something for everyone at every time of year: you can enjoy spring blossom in the cherry orchards and summer fun at the **Whitstable Oyster Festival**, walk the **Pilgrim's Way** across the North Downs in autumn, and keep the winter chill at bay with mulled wine and Victorian carols at the **Dickensian Christmas celebrations** in Rochester.

Kent has natural beauty from the iconic **White Cliffs of Dover** and the rolling chalk downs, to the salt marshes of the **Thames Estuary** and the wooded **Eden Valley** with its ancient castles. Archaeological sites and historic buildings tell the story of England: Iron Age burial barrows and Roman forts, Norman castles and moated Tudor manors, elegant Georgian town houses and Victorian railway stations. The cathedral city of **Canterbury** has been a centre of Christianity since the sixth century.

The White Cliffs of Dover iStock

Culture flourishes whether it's **Morris dancing** and pagan customs at the **Rochester Sweeps Festival**, opera in Royal Tunbridge Wells or modern art at **Margate's Turner Contemporary Gallery**.

Kent has enriched the English language, inspiring **Chaucer's Canterbury Tales** in the 14th century and prompting early attempts to standardise our spelling and grammar. **Shakespeare's** contemporary playwright and poet **Christopher Marlowe** was a Kentish man, while **William Blake** is said to have written *'Jerusalem'* after walking on the hills around **Shoreham**.

Charles Dickens grew up in Chatham, where his father was a naval clerk, and he set several of his novels on the moody marshes of Romney, in the Medway towns and on the windswept coast around Ramsgate. His comic creation Sam Weller has distinctly London/Kentish speech patterns and phrases. Dickens ended his days in Kent at Gad's Hill Place, and his life and work are celebrated at Eastgate House in Rochester, now a museum, where he wrote *The Pickwick Papers*.

John Buchanan wrote *The Thirty-Nine Steps* while convalescing in Broadstairs; **Noel Coward** penned *Blithe Spirit* when living at Romney Marsh; **E. Nesbit** based the station in *The Railway Children* on Halstead; **Richmal Crompton** created the *Just William* books when she was classics mistress at Bromley High School for Girls.

With its mild climate and fertile soil, Kent is known as **'The Garden of England'** and has provided fruit and vegetables, beer and cider to London for centuries. We still enjoy Kent apples and cherries though the orchards are decreasing in number. Hop-picking no longer provides Londoners with working holidays but Kent's breweries, like Britain's oldest, **Shepherd Neame** and new micro-breweries like **Moodley's** and **The Mad Cat**, are thriving with the trend for real ale. Folkestone and Whitstable provide high-quality fresh fish, and salt marsh lamb from the coastal region is highly prized by chefs and restaurateurs. You can try Kentish specialities in hundreds of country pubs, village teashops, seaside cafes and gourmet restaurants around the county.

The Kent coast and the River Medway made the county crucial to the nation's defence. Maritime history abounds from the Norman Cinque Ports with their ancient fortifications to the dockyards at Chatham and Rochester. The dockyards played a crucial part in maintaining our navy during World War II and the Battle of Britain raged in the skies over the Channel. **Sir Winston Churchill** gained his pilot's licence at Eastchurch on the Isle of Sheppey and Bomber Command protected the vital

navy installations at Sheerness from this airfield. **Biggin Hill** aerodrome near Bromley hosted the Operations Room for the flying bomb defences. Kent lost many of its sons and daughters in the armed forces and auxiliary services, including the Merchant Navy, in the two world wars.

Peacetime Kent became the Gateway to Europe with the opening of the Channel Tunnel in 1994 linking Folkestone and Calais. Eurotunnel to Paris and Lille has transformed the quiet town of Ashford and the new town of Ebbsfleet has grown around the busy international interchange.

iStock

Local Dialect

ARE YOU **DAPPY**, **DICKY** OR IN **DISABILE**? COLOURFUL PHASES YOU MAY COME ACROSS IN YOUR TRAVELS.

Kentish dialect is a rich mixture:

- Anglo-Saxon left its mark.
- Old French arrived on the coast with William the Conqueror.
- Hop-pickers brought a cockney influence and took Kentish expressions home.

A

Aching-Tooth – to wish for something very much. *'I've a terr'ble aching-tooth for a new horse.'*

Ackle – to make something mechanical work. *'I got my cycle to ackle all right after a good oiling.'*

Act the giddy goat – to act foolishly

Addle-headed – stupid; thoughtless

B

Bacca – tobacco

Bain't – are not. *'Surely you bain't agoin' yet-awhile?'*

Bannicking – a good hiding. *'Old Fred didn't half give his boy a bannicking for smashing that window.'*

Blustrous – blustering. *'A pretty blustrous wind.'*

Bobbery – a squabble, fuss

Brecky – breakfast, usually used by mothers to coax children. *'Hurry up with your brecky!'*

Bumblesome – awkward, clumsy, ill-fitting. *'That dress is much too bumblesome.'*

C

Cackle – to laugh, also talk as in *'cut the cackle'*

Chopbacks – fishermen (coastal area)

Clod-hoppers – large, heavy boots

Cow-crib – manger
Crummy – filthy, covered with vermin

D

Damping – to drizzle with rain, though not actually raining
Dappy – half-witted (West Kent)
Dead-alive – dull, stupid. 'It's a dead-alive place.'
Dicky – poorly, miserable. *'I had a dicky feeling and went to the doctor's.'*
Disabile – untidy dress. From the French déshabillé.
Dunnamany – don't know how many. *'I've told him dunnamany times.'*

E

Elevenses – a mid-morning drink or snack
Enow – enough
Eyesore – something which offends the eye, and spoils the appearance of a thing

F

Flitter-mouse – a bat
Fogo – a stink
Frig – to hop about, move in an erratic manner
Furriner – a 'foreigner'. i.e. someone from outside the parish

G

Gaffer – boss, master
Garp – stare, gawp
Glincey – slippery. *'The ice is terr'ble glincey.'*
Gogs – berries; goosegogs = gooseberries
Gollop – to eat or to drink greedily. *'Now don't you gollop your food!'*
Grizzle – to cry, whine especially children. *'Stop your grizzling!'*

H

Haffy-graffy – almost, near enough
Half moon – five bushel basket measures, especially for hops
Harkee – Listen!

Higgler – a middleman who goes round the country and buys up produce to sell and 'higgles' or haggles over the price.

I

Innards – intestines, guts; also an innings at cricket
Itch – to be very anxious

J

Jack-in-the-box –a reddish-purple flower, double polyanthus
July-bug – a brownish beetle, elsewhere called a cockchafer, which appears in July

K

Kibbered – cold and shivery. *'I were right kibbered today by the sea.'*
Kiddle – to tickle
Kink – to hitch, twist, get into a tangle
Kittens – the baskets in which fish are packed on the beach at Folkestone for transporting by train

to London and other markets

L

Leety – slow; slovenly
Lollop – to lounge about. *'The lazy boy just lollops about.'*
Longtails – 1. Pheasants.
2. Nickname for natives of Kent

M

Mannish – like a man; manly. *'He's a very mannish little fellow.'*
Measure for a new jacket – to beat, flog
Minnies – tearful, fed up; the miseries
Mushmalt – masculine looking, ugly woman

N

Narlie-wood – knotted wood, poor timber, useless for building (north-east Kent, Medway towns)
Ne'er a once – not once
Neighbour – to associate. 'Though

we live next door we don't neighbour.'

Nit – the egg of a louse. *'Dead as a nit'* is a common expression.

Nitty ninehairs – name given to a bald-headed man

Noration – a fuss, a row. *'What a noration there was!'*

O

Oast – a brick kiln for drying malt or hops

One-eyed – inconvenient, a general expression of disapproval. *'That's a middlin' one-eyed house.'*

Ornery – bad-tempered. *'She's an ornery old woman!'*

Out of doors – out of fashion. *'Her bonnet were right out of doors.'*

P

Palm-tree – the yew tree, associated with Palm Sunday

Partial – fond of. *'I be very partial to huffkins.'*

Peart – energetic

Polrumptious – rude; obstreperous

Pom – country produce including apples, possibly from the French pomme

Pom sarnie – apple jam sandwich

Plaguesome – troublesome

Punnet – a small basket, in which strawberries or other soft fruits are sold

Q

Queer – to puzzle. *'It queers me how it ever got there.'*

Queer Street – an awkward position, dire straits. *'He stole my money and left me in queer street.'*

Queezey – fearful or afraid; not too sure about a thing or person. *'That old house makes me feel real queezey.' 'I'm queezey about going out in the dark.'*

S

Salterns, saltings – salt marshes beyond the sea-walls

Sandwich – John Montagu, 4th Earl of Sandwich is said to have invented a portable snack for his hunting trips made of a slice of meat in bread. The idea caught on!

Scoff – to gobble; eat greedily

Scooning – to peep, pry. *'Now what be ye a-scooning about for in my shed?'*

Scrap – to fight, usually between children

Scrumping – stealing apples from an orchard

Shrockled – shrivelled, wrinkled, withered. *'A face like a shrockled apple.'*

Stodger – a sturdy fellow able to get about in all sorts of weather

Swimmy – giddy, faint

T

Taffety – squeamish; dainty; particular about food (East Kent)

Tally – a stick on which the number of bushels picked by the hop-picker is reckoned by the tallyman cutting a notch in it

Tatter – 1. fretful, unwell. *'Little Johnny be proper tatter today'*; 2. Cross, peevish, ill-tempered

Team – a litter of pigs or a brood of ducks

Tearful – an arduous or exacting job, *'This stone-quarryin' be a most tearful kind of job!'*

Thern – theirs; belonging to them. *'No taint ourn; that be thern!'* (North-East Kent and Medway towns)

Thick thumb'd – untidy; clumsy

Threddle – to thread a needle

Throws – a thoroughfare. The four-throws, a point where four roads meet, is a crossroads.

Thunderbugs – midges

Tickler – particular. *'I'll bet she's not that tickler.'*

Tiddy little thing – a very small thing

Tight up – to make tidy. *'My missus had gone to tight up.'*

Tissick – a tickling cough.

Truck – to have to do with. *'I never had much truck with drinking.'*

Trug – a kind of basket, much used by gardeners

Tumbling bay – a cascade, or small waterfall (West Kent)

Twink – a shrewish, grasping woman

Twitter – a state of agitation; a flutter. *'I'm all in a twitter.'*

U

Uck-up – a helping hand. *'Give us a uck-up with these sacks of taters, mate!'*

Umblement – a compliment

Uncle owl – a species of the fish, skate (Folkestone)

Unker-money – Monies paid for exceptionally dirty or unhealthy work – Chatham, Rochester, Strood, Royal Naval Dockyard workers

V

Vampishness – forwardness, perverseness

Vigilous – vicious, of a horse; fierce, angry

W

Wacker – someone or something beyond normal size or shape. *'That sow be a real wacker.'*

What cheer? – How are you doing? *'Wha'cher, mate?'*

Wiffle – to come in gusts of wind

Worrit – to worry

Y

Yellow stockings – when hop-leaves turn yellow

Yowl – to howl

Humour

The people of Kent have a droll sense of humour so let's share a few rib-tickling jokes

A Kent man and a Frenchman are discussing the Channel Tunnel.

The Frenchman says how wonderful it is that this co-operative venture has finally taken place, and that he never expected the English to go to such trouble to be united to the mainland of Europe. 'Mon Dieu,' he says, 'you Anglais 'ave worked so 'ard to get closer to your French brothers, I can 'ardly believe it!'

'Yes, it is strange,' says the Kentish man. 'You should have seen the trouble we had digging the Channel in the first place!'

A farmer was driving along a country road near the picturesque village of St Nicholas-at-Wade with a large load of fertiliser. A little boy, playing in front of his cottage, saw him and called out, 'What do you have on your truck?'

'Fertiliser,' the farmer replied.

'What are you going to do with it?' asked the little boy.

'Put it on strawberries,' answered the farmer.

'You ought to live here,' the little boy advised him. 'We put sugar and cream on ours.'

Two Bapchild Cricket Club players are chatting in the bar after a match. 'So did you have a hard time explaining last week's game to the wife?' says one.

'I certainly did,' says the other. 'She found out I wasn't there!'

An expectant father rang the Maternity Unit at the Medway Maritime Hospital to see how his wife, who had gone into labour, was getting on. By mistake, he was connected to the St Lawrence cricket ground.

'How's it going?' he asked.

'Fine,' came the answer. 'We've got three out and hope to have the rest out before lunch. The last one was a duck.'

A tourist is driving through Kent, when he passes a farmer standing in the middle of a huge field of hops. He pulls the car over and watches the farmer standing stock-still, doing absolutely nothing. Intrigued, the man walks over to the farmer and asks him, 'Excuse me sir, but what are you doing?'

The farmer replies, 'I'm trying to win a Nobel Prize.'

'How?' asks the puzzled tourist.

'Well,' says the farmer, 'I heard they give the prize to people who are outstanding in their field.'

Simon was down on his luck so he thought he would try getting a few odd jobs by calling at the posh houses on Wildernesse Estate in Sevenoaks. After a few 'no chances', a guy in one of the big houses thought he would give him a break and said, 'The porch needs painting so I'll give you £50 to paint it for me.'

'You're a life-saver, mister,' said Simon. 'I'll get started right away!'

Time passes until…

'There you go, I'm all done with the painting.'

'Well, here's your £50,' said the homeowner, handing over some crisp tenners.

'Thanks very much,' said Simon, pocketing the money. 'Oh and, by the way, it's a Ferrari, not a Porsche!'

'I can't believe it,' said the American tourist, looking at the grey skies over Broadstairs. 'I've been here an entire week and it's done nothing but rain. When do you guys get summer over here?'

'Well, that be hard to say, mister,' replied the elderly local. 'Last year, it were on a Wednesday.'

Many years ago there was a dispute between two villages, one in Kent and the other in Sussex. One day the Sussex villagers heard the cry, 'One man from Kent is stronger than one hundred Sussex men.'

The villagers in Sussex were furious and immediately sent their hundred strongest men to engage with the enemy. They listened, horrified by the screams and shouts. After hours of fighting, all was quiet but none of the men returned.

Later on, the same voice shouted out, 'Is that the best you can do?'

This fired up the people from Sussex and they rallied round, getting a thousand men to do battle. After days of the most frightful blood-curdling sounds, one man emerged from the battlefield, barely able to speak, but with his last breath he managed to murmur, 'It's a trap: there's two of them!'

"Knock, knock"

"Who's there?"

"Kent."

"Kent who?"

"Kent you tell by my voice?"

"My boat ran aground last week on the beach in Kent where the bouncing bomb was tested."

"Reculver?"

"Yes. I just waited for the next high tide."

"I went to an excellent sculpture exhibition in Kent yesterday."

"Maidstone?"

"No, they were all bronze."

"I took my family out for a picnic in Kent at the weekend."

"Ham and Sandwich?"

"No, scotch eggs and sausage rolls."

FUNNY PLACE NAMES IN KENT

BADGERS MOUNT

Balls Green

CLAP HILL

Ham, near Sandwich

HEARTS DELIGHT

Horneyman

PRATTS BOTTOM

Thong

TITSEY HILL

Recipes

Kent Lent Tart
Kentish Pudding Pie

This traditional pudding, rather like a baked cheesecake, was eaten all over Kent on Sundays during Lent. It was a favourite for Mothering Sunday.

Kent Lent Tart The Author

See **page 24** for recipe

Kent Huffkins

A HUFFKIN is a soft bread roll with a dent in the middle, traditionally baked all over Kent. The origin of the word is uncertain but one story claims it derives from a 16th-century baker's wife who, in a huff, poked the rising dough balls with her finger and told her husband to 'Get on and sell those!'

Kent Huffkins with a handy dent in the middle for jam and butter www.information-britain.co.uk

Ingredients:

700g (1½lb) plain flour

12g (½oz) yeast

1 teaspoonful castor sugar

1 ½ tsps salt

50g (2oz) lard

¾ pint (400ml) cold milk and warm water (or parsnip wine and warm water)

Preparation:

1. Sift the flour and salt and rub in the lard.

2. Cream the yeast and sugar in another basin.

3. Add the milk and water.

4. Pour this mixture onto the flour and make a light dough.

5. Stand in a warm place for 1 hour to rise.

6. Knead well.

7. Divide into twelve oval cakes about half-an-inch in thickness.

8. Make an indentation in the middle with your thumb.

9. Flour the cakes and place on a warm tin.

10. Leave in a warm place to prove until well risen.

11. Bake in a hot oven Gas Mark 7/220°C for 10 minutes or until brown.

12. Take out and wrap the cakes in a warm cloth to keep the crust soft.

13. Fill the hole with butter and Kent cherry jam if you have a sweet tooth or try fresh Kentish whelks seasoned with salt, pepper and vinegar.

Ginger Cobnut Cake

More cobnuts are grown in Kent than any other county iStock

COBNUTS are a type of hazelnut or filbert, first grown commercially in Kent in 1830 by a Mr Lambert.

Traditionally, cobnuts, like hops, were harvested by itinerant pickers from London. You may be able to buy fresh cobnuts, still in their husks, in early autumn; shell them and roast at a low temperature for one hour or buy dried, processed hazelnuts.

Ingredients:

200g (8oz) self-raising flour

1 rounded teaspoon of powdered ginger

100g (4oz) butter (at room temperature)

100g (4oz) brown sugar

50g (2oz) Kentish cobnuts, roasted and chopped

1 large egg, beaten

Preparation:

1. Sift flour and ginger into a bowl and rub in the butter.

2. Add the sugar and nuts.

3. Mix in the beaten egg.

4. Turn into a greased cake tin.

5. Bake in a pre-warmed oven at Gas Mark 4/180°C for 20 minutes.

6. Serve warm with cream or Kentish apple compote.

Kent Lent Tart/Kentish Pudding Pie

Ingredients:

SHORTCRUST PASTRY

150g (6oz) plain flour
75g (3oz) butter, chilled
3–4 tbsp cold water
1 pinch salt

1. Make the pastry either by hand or in a food processor.
2. Roll out and line an 8″ flan tin, prick the base, and refrigerate for 20 minutes.
3. Bake blind (use ceramic beans to keep the pastry flat) at Gas Mark 4/180°C for 15 minutes until cooked, but not brown.

FILLING

285ml (½ pint) milk
25g (1oz) ground rice
75g (3oz) butter at room temperature
50g (2oz) caster sugar
2 eggs
Zest of **1** lemon
½ tsp nutmeg
1 bay leaf
25g (1oz) currants

Preparation:

1. Put the rice, milk and bay leaf into a non-stick pan and bring to the boil, stirring until the rice thickens to a custard-like constituency.

2. Put aside to cool while you make the rest of the filling.

3. Cream together the butter and sugar until pale and fluffy.

4. Beat in the eggs.

5. Add the lemon zest, nutmeg and rice mixture.

6. Pour into the pastry case.

7. Scatter currants and more nutmeg on top.

8. Bake in a hot oven at Gas Mark 6/200°C for 10 minutes.

9. Reduce the temperature to Gas Mark 2/150°C and bake for 20 minutes until the filling is set.

10. Serve warm with cream if desired.

Lees Court, Sheldwich British Library

BROTHERLY RIVALRY, SHELDWICH 1655

George and **Freeman Sondes** were born into a wealthy family near Faversham in the 1630s. It was customary in Kent for estates to be divided equally between male heirs but a hundred years earlier the Sondes family had sought a special Act of Parliament to avoid splitting the land, so the youngest son, Freeman, would have no inheritance. George was set fair to inherit 6,500 acres and two fine manor houses – Town Place, Throwley, and Lees Court, Sheldwich.

The boys' father, Sir George, made it clear that George, who was growing up handsome and popular with the ladies, would inherit, while Freeman must find a profession. Freeman resented his unequal treatment and became increasingly sullen and unsociable, taking solace in gambling. Their father began to favour George even more. Father and younger son quarrelled and came to blows.

Freeman decided to rid himself of his brother. On 7 August 1655 the Assizes were coming to Maidstone, which meant the town constables would be busy. The Sondes family were all at Lees Court. On Sunday 5 August Freeman crept into the kitchen, took a meat cleaver and hid it. On the Monday night, while Sir George and his eldest son slept, Freeman took the cleaver and a dagger and crept into his brother's room. Freeman struck him on the side of the head with the heavy cleaver, cracking his skull but not killing him. As his brother writhed in agony, he struck him five more times. Blood and bone flew everywhere but George clung to life. Freeman was consumed with regret, revolted by his actions, but it was too late – George was mortally wounded. Freeman put his brother out of his misery with a dagger to his heart, then went to his father, hands all bloody, and confessed, *'Father, I have killed my brother.'*

His father replied, *'Why then you must look to be hanged.'*

Sir George called a Justice, who took Freeman into the stinking 'common prison' at Maidstone. Freeman pleaded guilty to murder and on 21 August 1655 he was hanged on the hill at Penenden Heath. His body was buried at Holy Cross Church, Bearsted, while the brother he murdered rests in the churchyard at St Michael and All Angels, Throwley.

THE BODY ON THE BEACH, RAMSGATE 1859

A 5.45am on 11 April 1859, the naked body of a man in his thirties was found at the sea's edge in Ramsgate, precipitating a frenzy of speculation. The man's left hand had been hacked off and there was a single stab wound to his chest. Some clothes lay nearby, the pockets empty. The Harbour Police were called and found the severed hand, with several fingers missing, a torn shirt and a hatchet some distance away among the rocks.

An inquest took place the next day and the Ramsgate Gazette appealed for someone to identify the dead man and raised the possibility of a murderous lunatic at large. People wondered whether the victim had fallen from the cliffs, been washed ashore or thrown from a boat.

The deceased was identified by staff at The Royal Oak Hotel on Harbour Parade as a foreign gentleman who spoke English poorly, wore a gold watch and signet ring and had a portemonnaie full of sovereigns when he'd paid his bill. Further enquiries revealed that on the Sunday the man had visited a local 'dressmaker' of easy virtue and boasted about the cash in his possession. In the evening, he had drunk some ale alone at The Crown Inn, Broadstairs.

Later, police discovered that he was a German on holiday who had arrived in Southampton from America at the end of March. The inquest re-opened and many Ramsgate shopkeepers and residents came forward to report sightings of the mystery man, including the 'dressmaker' and a young couple who were the last to see the victim walking near the East Cliff Promenade. Superintendent Pritchard from the Harbour Police presented the hatchet, clothes and a note in German which read, *'Dear mother, Here is five dollars – little, but from a good heart, Henry Matterigh.'*

An anonymous letter to The Times on 7 May suggested a conspiracy to rob the German, possibly involving the lady of ill-repute. Other correspondents suggested corruption on the part of the police and medical practitioners. At the end of May, news came from New York identifying the man as a Frederick Mattern, a respectable butcher who had lost several fingers in a sausage machine; the note had been written by his brother for their mother in Germany. It was decided that Mattern had somehow lost his money and committed suicide in despair, his property being stolen afterwards by an opportunist. The case remains officially unsolved.

THE SEAL CHART MURDER, IGHTHAM 1908

On 24 August 1908, at about 2.30pm, **Major-General Luard** and his wife, **Caroline**, left their home in Ightham, near Sevenoaks, and went for a walk with their dog. The Major-

Dawn at Ramsgate Harbour iStock

General, a former Royal Engineer, wished to retrieve his golf clubs from Godden Green Golf Club, while Mrs Luard wanted some exercise before returning home to give Mrs Stewart, the wife of a local solicitor, afternoon tea. About a mile along the road, by St Lawrence's Church in the village of Seal Chart, they parted company at a wicket gate that led to a 'bungalow summerhouse' known as La Casa. Beyond the summerhouse was a path through the woods, which would allow Mrs Luard to return home in good time for her visitor.

Major-General Luard collected his clubs at 4.05pm and got a lift home from the local vicar to find Mrs Stewart still awaiting the return of his wife. Luard set off to search the woodland route and reached the summerhouse, which was locked and empty, at about 5.15pm. On the veranda lay the body of Caroline Luard. She had been shot in the head and her three rings and purse were missing. No cartridges were found at the scene, merely some 'disappearing footprints'.

The time of Mrs Luard's murder was estimated to be 3.15pm, when Major-General Luard was walking towards the Golf clubhouse. Three shots were heard at that time by two local residents. Scotland Yard was called in to investigate with two bloodhounds, named Sceptre and Solferino, to sniff out the killer's escape route; the trail went cold at the main road.

After the initial inquest, a whispering campaign began accusing Major-General Luard of the murder and he received vitriolic anonymous letters. He left Ightham and went to stay with Colonel Warde, the local MP and Chief Constable. On 17 September Luard walked to the railway line at Teston and jumped in front of the 9.09 train to Tonbridge.

The idea that the murderer was an opportunist thief, a gypsy, hop-picker or itinerant, was rejected; the police were convinced Mrs Luard knew her killer. Suspicion fell on a convicted murderer called John Dickman who was believed to have defrauded the lady when she sent him charitable help in the form of a cheque. Dickman's original conviction was considered unsafe but his appeal failed. Some claimed that the judge who tried Dickman, the Appeal Court judges, and the Home Secretary, Winston Churchill, who refused to commute his death sentence, were all friends of Major-General Luard bent on avenging his and his wife's deaths. Caroline Luard's murderer was never conclusively identified.

Place Names

The county of Kent has more than its fair share of quaint and quirky place names to pique the traveller's curiosity and fire the imagination.

Most Kentish names go back to the Domesday Book and beyond and are derived from Old English, Anglo-Saxon and Celtic dialects. The meaning of some names is obvious: *Sevenoaks* did indeed once boast seven oak trees and was first mentioned around AD 1100 as *Seouenaca*. Others are more obscure: *Hartlip* in Swale, first mentioned in the 11th century as *Heordlyp*, is said to mean *'fence that deer leap over'*, from the Old English *hliep* for a gate or fence and *heorot*, a stag or hart. *Borstal*, near Rochester, gets its name from the Anglo-Saxon *burg-steal*, a place of refuge. It was the

One of the original oak trees? Knole Park in Sevenoaks
iStock

location of a youth prison, which gave its name to the Borstal reform school system in the mid-twentieth century.

Other names are based on landscape: *Blackheath* speaks for itself; *Sittingbourne* refers to a place by a

Blackheath looks rather green in this aerial photo Mark Fosh

'*bourne*' or *clear stream*; *Sandwich* meant '*a sandy harbour*', not a tasty snack, though it is conveniently near *Ham*. *Plucks Gutter*, near Ramsgate, dates back to 1530 when this stretch of the River Stour was given the nickname after a Dutchman called Mr Pluck who drained the surrounding land.

Some place names conjure up all manner of intriguing images: did the original inhabitants of *Thong* favour skimpy lingerie? Might their outfits have had an effect on the natives of *Horneyman* or *Pett Bottom*? Would the good ladies of *Womenswold*, just off the A2, have disapproved? Maybe the women of *Loose*, near Maidstone, did approve!?

You might wonder if *Stiff Street* near Sittingbourne has an unusually

Not so fast! A road sign at Thong. Ryan Jones

high number of funeral parlours or if the local constabulary all live in *Cop Street* near Faversham. Is *Frogs Tough* in Boxley a hangout for rough amphibians? Do posh rodents live in *Rats Castle*, Biddenden? Do the villagers of *Monkery*, near Bethersden, get up to mischief or do they live a monastic life? Is it chilly in *Cooling*?

Kemsing, a stopping place along the Pilgrim's Way on the North Downs, has an area quaintly named *Noah's Ark*, while Benenden boasts two hamlets with biblical names: *Little Nineveh* and *Great Nineveh*. *Golgotha* sounds sinister but is home to The East Kent Light Railway tunnel built to serve the Kent coalfield.

Estate agents must find it easier to sell homes in *Hearts Delight*, near Sittingbourne, than in *Horrid Hill*, Gillingham or *Grubb Street*, Dartford.

Wouldn't you prefer to live in exotic *Palmtree Downs* in Barham than the uninvitingly named *Deadman's Wood*? Langley Heath offers the uncomfortable-sounding *Gravelly Bottom Road*.

Do the locals in *Mockbeggar*, near Norton Ash, make fun of homeless people?

You must be able to eat and drink in *The Guzzle* at Brasted but can you float on *Cork's Pond*, Tunbridge Wells?

Further Quarter, near Tenterden, just sounds too far away.

Walks

MARGATE WALK

See map on inside front cover.

This short walk around Margate will give you a taste for this flourishing seaside town, taking in some of the new as well as the well established attractions and buildings that are steeped in local history.

THE BASICS

DISTANCE: 2 Miles

MINIMUM TIME TO WALK: 1½ hours or all morning if you dawdle

PATHS: Pavements, flat

DOG FRIENDLY: Town centre walk, not really suitable

STARTING POINT: Margate Station or Town Car Park

If you have travelled by train then the station is where this walks starts but if you are already parked in one of the many car parks in Margate then pick up the walk from the nearest point and follow the route indicated; it's more or less circular!

Arlington house and surfboat memorial Pam Fray

As you head out of the station on Station Approach, look back and admire the station building, designed and built in the mid 1920s by Maxwell Fry in the classic Roman Baths style that was popular in that period. Head towards Marine Terrace where you will see the memorial to

Clock Tower Andrew-Longton

As you walk along Marine Terrace you will pass the vast expanse of Dreamland Amusement Park with its classic rides and entertainment. Perhaps return after this stroll around the town.

On your left are the renowned Margate Sands.

Further along Marine terrace you will come to The Clock Tower, a 21m (70 ft) high tower built to commemorate Queen Victoria's Golden Jubilee in 1887.

Bear left onto Marine Drive and onto The Parade. You cannot fail to see the impressive Turner Contemporary Gallery, built on the site where Turner is said to have stayed during his visits in 1820 -30. The gallery has a varied programme of exhibitions of contemporary works and some commemorative Turner works. For details visit **www.turnercontemporary.org**

the crew from the Margate Lifeboat who died during a storm in 1897. And nearby is Nayland Rock Shelter where T S Elliot wrote in 1921.

The Stone Pier iStock

As you face Turner Contemporary, on your left is the Stone Pier, built between 1810 - 1820, the pier replaced an earlier wooden pier. There are some interesting buildings here for you explore.

The Droit House, originally built for harbour administration, is now used as the Visitor Information Centre for Margate, Broadstairs and Ramsgate. For more details, visit **www.visitthanet.co.uk**

The Shell Lady ©Ann Carrington

after Turners Landlady; she is forever looking out to sea, waiting for his return.

Retrace your steps back down the pier and head on up Fort Hill and along Fort Crescent to explore the famous Winter Gardens; built in 1911, they have outlived several rivals and hosted many well known acts and bands, including The Beatles, who, in 1963 gave 2 performances a day for 6 days.

Leave the Winter Gardens and head down Trinity Square and then on to Trinity Hill where at the junction of King Street you will come across The Tudor House on your left.

The Tudor House is now a museum but originally it was a farmhouse on the edge of Margate Town. Stay a while and learn about Margate's fascinating past.

Along the pier are former coal bunkers that have been converted for modern leisure use. At the end of the pier is a bronze called *The Shell Lady*,

From The Tudor House, carry on down Trinity Hill and turn right onto Love Lane. Love Lane, Duke Street and King Street are all part of the old town with a rich array of buildings dating back to the 16th century. Now a thriving creative hub, in the 1960s the area was very nearly demolished.

At the end of Duke Street turn left and left again onto Market Street which in turn becomes Lombard Street. This area is blessed with a selection of galleries and museums for you to dip into as the mood takes you.

At the end of Lombard Street, turn right onto Hawley Street where you will pass India House, which was built in the late 1760s for Captain John Gould who was one of the first returnees from India to 'retire by the seaside' in Margate.

Carry on down Hawley Street to Cecil Square said to be the first square in England built outside London. Take a few minutes to explore Cecil Square and then go back to Hawley Street and turn right onto Cecil Street. It is a short walk down to Hawley Square with a fine selection of terraced houses overlooking a small park.

Walk to the end of Hawley Square and you will come across the Theatre Royal Margate, a grade II listed theatre built in 1786 and still in use today with a varied programme of performances. Visit **www.theatreroyalmargate.com** for details.

From the Theatre Royal, if you came by rail you can retrace your steps to Cecil Square and then on to Marine Gardens and back to the station. Or, having had a taster of what Margate has to offer, carry on exploring on your own.

ROCHESTER CITY WALK

See map on inside back cover.

A circular walk taking in the cathedral, castle and Charles Dickens' haunts – there's so much to see you could take all day.

THE BASICS

DISTANCE: 1½ miles (2.5km)

STARTING POINT: From the Station or Station car park

MINIMUM TIME TO WALK: 1½ hours or all day if you dawdle

PATHS: Pavements, flat

DOG FRIENDLY: Town centre walk, not really suitable

TOILETS: Castle Gardens or the Tourist Information Centre

From the railway station or station car park, turn right onto High Street and follow until you reach the junction with Star Hill. Cross over onto Eastgate and follow until you reach Crow Lane.

Restoration House Alamy Stock Images

Turn left down Crow Lane until you reach Restoration House, where Charles II stayed in June 1660 on the eve of his coronation. Opposite Restoration House is an entrance to The Vines, described by Samuel Pepys in 1667 as 'a pretty seat'.

Take the diagonal path along The Vines until it joins Vines Lane, bear right on Vines Lane and at a T junction, bear right onto St Margarets Street, past King's Rochester School/Satis House, the model for Miss Havisham's home in Dickens' Great Expectations.

The High Street Saltaire Alamy Stock Images

Rochester Cathedral iStock

Then bear right onto Boley Hill and on to Rochester Cathedral, the second oldest cathedral in England, founded by Bishop Justus in AD 604. Take some time to look around this wonderful building. Then cross into the Castle Gardens; you can tour Rochester Castle with its 113-foot (34m) Norman keep.

Eastgate Danny Robinson

Guildhall Museum Chris Whippet

To continue, look for Castle Hill just to the right of the castle car park. Follow Castle Hill down to the Esplanade, turn right and stay on the right hand side of the road and follow until you reach the junction of the A2 and where it joins with the pedestrianised section of the High Street. Walk back up the High Street with its pubs and cafes, drop in at the Guildhall Museum, which houses a replica of a convict hulk, Six Poor Travellers House and Eastgate House. Follow High Street and keep ahead onto Eastgate and then retrace your steps back to the station or car park.

If you choose to park in the castle or the cathedral car parks, you can easily pick up the route from the map and follow it until you return to your chosen start point.

Ghost Stories

TALES OF THE SUPERNATURAL TO CHILL THE BLOOD

Kent's rolling hills, ancient castles and quaint villages harbour more than their fair share of ghosts and ghouls. The creaking timbers of the local inns hide restless spirits; shadowy figures glide along castle battements; unearthly cries echo in the grey stone churchyards. Lost souls reach out to the living to tell their stories, Kent's unseen history.

THE UNHAPPY GHOSTS OF HEVER CASTLE

Merchant's son **Thomas Bullen** had high ambitions for his family. He changed his surname to **Boleyn**, moved his aristocratic wife **Elizabeth Howard**, daughter of the Duke of

Hever Castle, childhood home of Anne Boleyn iStock

Norfolk, into 13th-century Hever Castle, and started grooming his daughters to make advantageous marriages. Daughter **Anne** surpassed his expectations by capturing the heart

Anne Boleyn in an engraving by Henry Thomas Ryall (1811 – 1867). Digital restoration by Steven Wynn Photography.

of **King Henry VIII**, who divorced his wife, split with the Church of Rome and risked his kingdom to marry her in 1533.

However, Anne's vivacious wit and charm were not enough to make up for her failure to give the king a son and heir. With only a daughter – the future **Queen Elizabeth I** – from his controversial marriage, Henry and his advisors began to plot Anne's downfall. Her greedy, scheming family didn't help matters and soon Anne was in the Tower of London accused of witchcraft, adultery, incest and treason. On 19 May 1536, the 35-year-old queen was beheaded with a sword while Henry hunted in Richmond Park. He married lady-in-waiting **Jane Seymour** the very next day.

With such a tumultuous life, it is not surprising that Anne Boleyn seems unable to rest in peace. Her ghost is one of the most frequently spotted in

England with 30,000 sightings at 120 locations; Hever Castle is no exception. The unfortunate queen returns to the grounds of the home where she spent a happy childhood and from which she embarked upon an adventure that changed the course of English history. She can be glimpsed drifting silently across the bridge that spans the River Eden, from whence she roams the castle gardens until dawn. Christmas Eve is apparently the best time to spot her but witnesses vary on whether she still has her head or is carrying it under her arm.

Anne Boleyn's spectre has company at Hever Castle, including an unknown unhappy ghost who wanders the corridors, groaning and banging, and a phantom horse that gallops through the long gallery.

THE BLUE BELL HILL GHOST

Kent's ghosts are not all ancient. The A229 at **Blue Bell Hill** is haunted by a young woman and a girl aged about ten. Some say the woman was a bride-to-be out on her hen night with some girlfriends in 1965 when their car was involved in a fatal collision near the bridge over the Old Chatham Road; others speak of a young girl mowed down by a hit-and-run driver at the site. Over the decades, many unsuspecting motorists have reported a vanishing woman hitch-hiker on this stretch of road or a female pedestrian who steps in front of their car only to disappear without a trace.

In the early of hours of 13 July 1974, a bricklayer from Rochester called **Maurice Goodenough** was driving through Blue Bell Hill, when a child jumped in front of his car. *'The girl just walked out in front of me,'* he said. *'My car hit her with a hell of a bang.'* Maurice stopped and found the girl lying in the road, with a cut to her forehead and grazes on her knees. He covered her with a blanket then he rushed off to Rochester Police Station to report what had happened. They returned to the scene to find nothing but the blanket. The police searched the area with tracker dogs, but no scent, tracks or blood could be found. Goodenough's car was undamaged. A newspaper appeal for the missing girl and a check on hospital admissions proved fruitless. Still shaken from the experience, Goodenough was interviewed by the News of the World. *'I'm not going mad,'* he said. *'But where did she vanish?'*

In 1992, late on a Sunday evening in November, a 54-year-old coach driver, Ian Sharpe, was on his way home to Maidstone, when a young woman appeared in front of his vehicle near the Aylesford turn-off on the A229. The woman stared strangely right into his eyes before he hit her and her body fell under the car. Mortified, he slammed on his brakes, and jumped out to help the woman. *'I honestly thought I had killed her,'* he told the local press. *'I was so scared to look underneath, but I knelt down and looked – there was nothing there.'* He went to Rochester police to report the incident and they returned to the scene with him but found nothing. A month later, two motorists reported hitting a woman wearing a red scarf, near the Robin Hood Lane junction at Blue Bell Hill. They also searched and informed police but, yet again, no body was found.

THE GHOSTS OF PLUCKLEY

Pluckley holds the Guinness Book of Records title for **'Most Haunted Village in England'** and has featured in several TV shows investigating the paranormal. Ghost-hunters have spotted the mournful **Red Lady** who sobs as she wanders round St Nicholas's churchyard looking for the grave of her unchristened baby. The ghost is believed to be that of the wife of one of the Derings, lords of the

The Dering Arms, one of the Haunted Pubs of Pluckley iStock

manor of Pluckley, whose tiny child was buried hastily in an unmarked grave.

Another popular village ghost is **The Screaming Man**, believed to be a bricklayer who fell to his death while at work. There is also the shadowy figure of a highwayman who was pinioned to a tree with a sword thrust at **Fright Corner**, as it is now known.

The ghost of an elderly woman, who accidentally set herself on fire, haunts Pluckley, as does the schoolmaster, who hanged himself in the 1800s and now walks round the village wearing his favourite frock coat and striped trousers.

Perhaps the most active ghost of all is that of **Edward Brett** at Elvey Farm. In 1900, he gave a penny to each of his children and fifteen shillings to his wife, then went calmly into the dairy and shot himself. Mr Brett has since been seen many times around the farm, now a hotel, walking the corridors. One hotel guest spotted him lying on a bed; other guests report a strange smell like burning hay or hearing a voice whispering in the dairy where Brett died.

THE GHOSTS OF DOVER CASTLE

Dover Castle was built in the 12th century to protect England's shores from marauding pirates. In the 18th century, it kept out Napoleon's army and in World War II it became an underground command centre, frequented by Prime Minister Winston Churchill. The castle also boasts a number of apparitions.

Dover Castle – a busy place for the paranormal iStock

Haunted tunnels? Fort Amherst, Chatham by David Pearson

THE HAUNTED TUNNELS OF FORT AMHERST

Originally built in 1756 to defend London from French invasion, **Fort Amherst**, with its labyrinth of tunnels in the cliffs, is now a military history attraction. Tourists visiting the fortress report hearing the sounds of children crying, a woman wailing, voices whispering in their ears, and seeing flickering dark shadows even in the daytime. Visitors have often found small handprints on their backs on leaving the tunnels, as if they'd been touched by a child. The apparition of a soldier has been witnessed in the lower gun floor, though he only appears to staff and regular visitors.

Local Customs

ANCIENT AND MODERN TRADITIONS CREATE EXCITING EVENTS TO VISIT IN KENT

'Stand fast twig, bear well top,
God send thee a yowling crop,
Every twig, apples big,
Every bough, apples enow.
Hats full! Caps full!
Half bushel bags full!
And my pockets full too! Huzzah!'

TRADITIONAL CIDER SONG

The Yowling ensured a good apple harvest and cider-making iStock

THE YOWLING

Known outside Kent as **the Wassail**, it derives from pagan times. Wassail or *'Wass Hal'* means *'Be Thou of Good Health'*. The time of the wassail varied from Christmas Eve to Twelfth Night. Local people would promenade into the orchards carrying jugs of cider and creating a great deal of noise by banging pots and pans. They would drink to the good health of the trees and the next year's crop, then, when they had drunk their fill, they would pour the remaining cider around the tree roots. Wheat flour cakes were eaten at these ceremonies and small pieces of the cake were dipped in cider and placed in the forks of the trees as

A Morris dancer with a basketry hobby horse at the Sweeps festival in front of Rochester Cathedral. Clem Rutter

a thanksgiving to the spirit of the tree. There's still plenty of cider-tasting to be done in Kent.

THE SWEEPS FESTIVAL

Dating back to ancient pagan spring celebrations, this festival took place every year on the first weekend in May when traditionally chimney sweeps were able to leave the soot behind and have some fun. Originally, the festival would begin with the **Jack-in-the-Green ceremony**, when the young sweeps 'woke' a seven-foot character at dawn on Blue Bell Hill, Chatham. The Jack-in-the-Green would walk with the chimney sweeps in their parade through the town of Rochester. When the Climbing Boys' Act 1868 made it illegal to employ young boys to carry out the trade, the traditional procession gradually died out and the final May celebration was held in the early 1900s. However, the festival has been revived in Rochester and is now in its thirty-fourth year. The event includes the parade of the sweeps with their blackened faces, Kentish music and Morris dancing.

Morris dancers do plenty of footwork at the Sweeps Festival in Rochester iStock

WHITSTABLE OYSTER FESTIVAL AND THE BLESSING OF THE WATERS

Getting ready for Grotter-building in Whitstable iStock

The festival takes place in Whitstable, the most prominent oyster-trading centre in England, every summer around St James' Day, which is celebrated on 25 July. St James of Compostela is the patron saint of the oyster trade and the oystermen and their families offer thanks for the bounty of the sea. The festival, which dates back to Norman times, takes place in the evening on Reeves Beach and ends with a firework display.

GROTTER-BUILDING

Part of the ancient Oyster Festival, this traditionally uses up the thousands of shells left over after a week of oyster shucking. Grotters, or mounds

Whitstable Beach and fishing huts iStock

of sand, are built across the beach and decorated with oyster shells. Originally built by children who would beg 'a penny for the grotter', much as other children did for Guy Fawkes, today's grotters are built purely for the fun of it and lit by candles to produce an intriguing night-time spectacle.

THE HOODEN HORSE

This East Kent custom, involving men and boys dressing up and taking wooden hobbyhorses from house to house, has pagan roots and takes place in midwinter by custom.

In 1909 Percy Maylam reported:

… the horse … ('Hoodener') … assumes a most restive manner … doing his best to unseat the 'Rider', who tries to mount him, while the 'Waggoner' shouts 'whoa' … 'Mollie' … is a lad dressed up in women's clothes and vigorously sweeps the ground behind the horse with a birch broom. There are generally two or three performers besides , who play the concertina, tambourine or instruments of that kind … Beer and largesse are distributed …

In 1828 a Broadstairs woman was reported to have been frightened to death by the Hooadeners and magistrates banned the custom. It has now been successfully revived with no further casualties.

GOING CHAMPIONING

Like wassailing, this involved boys and men going around singing carols at Christmas and being given beer and mulled wine by householders. It is probably connected with St George the Champion, a leading character in the Mummers play.

THE IVY GIRL AND THE HOLLY BOY

It was the custom on Shrove Tuesday in West Kent to create two figures in the form of a boy and girl, one made of holly, the other of ivy. A group of girls busied themselves in one part of the village in burning the holly boy, which they had stolen from the boys, while the boys were to be found in another part of the village burning the ivy girl, which they had stolen from the girls. The ceremony, an old pagan one given Christian significance, was accompanied by loud huzzas.

The Holly and the Ivy: pagan symbols adopted by Christianity iStock

Local Sports
AND GAMES

The local pub is still the focus for many traditional sports. In Kent you can work up a thirst with skittles or historic team games

---

'We are coming to take your land,
We are the Rovers,
We are coming to take your land,
Though you are the guardian soldiers.

'We don't care for your men nor you,
Though you are the Rovers,
We don't care for your men nor you,
For we are the guardian soldiers.'

TRADITIONAL SINGING GAME,
WROTHAM, KENT

RED ROVER

Variants of this outdoor game, which is a little like British Bulldog, are played throughout the United Kingdom.

Some say the game goes back to the Viking raids but the Kentish version is believed to have originated during the threat of a Napoleonic invasion. Participants link hands and form two lines, about thirty feet apart, one representing the invaders, one the defenders. Teams alternate chanting verses of the song with each verse introducing a new element. Players are called out by name, one at a time, and

Teenagers Playing Red Rover Kyra Malicse

have to run at the line and try to break the chain until only one player is left. There's a fair bit of physical contact and injuries are not unheard of!

'There came three dukes a-riding,
a-riding, ride, ride, riding;
There came three dukes a-riding,
With a tinsy, tinsy, tee!

'Come away, fair lady, there is
no time to spare;
Let us dance, let us sing,
Let us join the wedding ring.'

THREE DUKES

This singing game is a little gentler than Red Rover and has many variations throughout Great Britain. The Kent version requires players to form two lines and skip under an arch formed by the raised arms of a player from each side. Actions may be added to match the lyrics.

KICK UP JENNY

This game was once played in every public house in Kent, with wooden ninepins and a leaden ball. The ball is fastened to a cord suspended from the ceiling, exactly over the centre pin. When skilfully handled, the ball is swung from the length of the cord, so as to bring down all the pins at once. The game has enjoyed a small revival recently.

Ninepins are smaller than skittles iStock

MATCH-RUNNING

A form of foot racing, also known as match-a-running and stroke-bias, is peculiar to Kent, and resembles another traditional game called Prisoner's Base. It was popular in the 17th century when men and women from one parish were paired with runners from a neighbouring parish. The runners had to hit their partner seven times during the race.

BAT AND TRAP

This team game is something of a Kent tradition and isn't really known outside the county. Some have suggested that it is the ancestor of cricket with eight players on each side taking turns to bowl and bat or field. A hard rubber ball is placed on one end of a 'trap', which is a low wooden box 22 inches (560mm) long and 5 inches wide (130mm), on top of which is a simple see-saw

Playing bat and Trap Nigel Chadwick

Playing bat and Trap Nigel Chadwick

mechanism. Each player in turn hits the opposite end of the see-saw lever (the 'striker') with the bat to propel the ball into the air, and then, using the same bat, attempts to hit the ball between two 7-foot (2.1m) high posts at the other end of the pitch. The trap is hinged at one end and fielders must use the ball to knock this 'wicket' flat to bowl out the batsman. Although the games are obviously related and bat and trap does seem to be a more primitive version of cricket, the assumed split must have happened many centuries ago and is lost in time. First played around Canterbury in the 14th century, bat and trap had almost died out when, in 1922, a pub league was formed and the game became popular once again.

STOOLBALL

The Little Pretty Pocket Book by Isaiah Thomas (1767) depicts men playing stoolball Creative Commons

This team sport, which dates back to at least the 15th century, originated in Sussex but has been popular in Kent for hundreds of years. Like bat and trap, it has been suggested that it is resembles cricket as well as baseball and rounders; in fact stoolball is sometimes called 'cricket in the air'. Traditionally, it was played by milkmaids, who used their milking stools as a 'wicket', and it is still mainly a woman's game though teams can be ladies only or mixed. There are ladies' leagues in Sussex, Surrey and Kent and mixed leagues in Sussex, and the game has Sports Council recognition.

Village greens like this one at Littlebourne are the perfect place for playing traditional games Paul Hensman

Local History

Kent's rich history is revealed in every town and hillside...

ANCIENT STONES AND BARROWS

The earliest inhabitants of Kent left their mark at Swanscombe in the Palaeolithic Era some 400,000 years ago (you can visit the Swanscombe Heritage Park and nature reserve). Their Iron Age descendants created the Medway Megaliths, burial chambers marked by stone structures near the River Medway, the best preserved being the Coldrum Stones and the Chestnuts Long Barrow.

THE ROMANS: FORTS AND VILLAS

Julius Caesar invaded Kent in 55 BC and easily defeated the indigenous tribes, though the Romans did not establish themselves in the region until AD 43. After a century of trading between Rome and what we now call England, Emperor Claudius decided to take advantage of the quarrels between the rival local princes and landed his troops in Richborough, near Sandwich, where a Roman Fort still stands. Emperor Carausius went on to build the fort at Regulbium (Reculver) in the third century, where the striking twin towers of a 12th-century church now stand within the Roman foundations. More evidence of Roman civilisation survives in the form of the Lullingstone Roman Villa at Eynsford, discovered in 1939, and the third-century Roman Painted House now in its own museum in New Street, Dover.

THE NORMAN CONQUEST: KEEPS AND CASTLES

When Duke William of Normandy landed in England in 1066 and defeated King Harold, he and his army had a long journey through Kent to claim the throne in London. He faced extreme hostility from locals and Kent proclaimed itself *invicta*, meaning 'unconquered'. William the Conqueror, as he became known, made his half-brother, Odo, the Earl of Kent. Odo seized vast lands for himself and his family until the people of Kent rebelled against his unjust behaviour in 1067.

Although Odo only ruled Kent for a few months, the Normans left a long-lasting impression, creating the Cinque Ports ('five ports') – Hythe, Dover, New Romney and Sandwich in Kent plus Hastings in Sussex. In the 12th century castles were built at Canterbury, Dover and Rochester, the last of which boasts a fine Norman keep constructed from the ruins of the Roman city walls. There are also castle ruins at Dane John Mound in Canterbury and Sutton Valence, with its splendid views over the Weald.

THE MEDIEVAL KENT: WARS, PLAGUE AND THE POWER OF THE CHURCH

Christianity had been brought to England by Saint Augustine, a missionary who landed on the island of Thanet in AD 597 and founded an abbey in the capital of the Kingdom of Kent, Cantwara or Canterbury. A cathedral was built on the site between 1070 and 1077. Archbishop Thomas Becket's murder in the cathedral in 1170 by Henry II's men made Canterbury a popular place of pilgrimage, as depicted in Chaucer's Canterbury Tales two centuries later. The cathedral was rebuilt in Gothic style after a fire in 1174 and again in its present form in the late 14th century.

The 13th century was marked by long wars with France and sieges of Kent's main castles – Rochester in 1215 and Dover from 1216 to 1217. More Anglo-French conflict began in 1337 with the Hundred Years War.

Between 1348 and 1350, the Black Death killed nearly half Kent's population. War and plague left few to work the land, and starvation and poverty led to rebellions in agricultural communities. The most notable uprising was the disastrous Peasants' Revolt in 1381, led by Wat Tyler.

THE TUDORS AND STUARTS

As the Plantagenets then the Tudors fought for control of England in the 14th and 15th centuries, aristocrats built fortified manor houses across Kent like the moated Ightham Mote and Penshurst Place near Tunbridge Wells. Henry VIII's break with the Catholic Church and plundering of the monasteries put wealth and power into the hands of new families like the Boleyns at Hever Castle. Henry himself stayed at Chartwell, near Westerham, when he was courting Anne Boleyn; much later it became the home of wartime prime minister, Sir Winston Churchill until his death in 1965.

In 1642 the Civil War between Royalists and Parliamentarians began and Kent, like the rest of England, was in turmoil. In 1649, King Charles I was executed and Oliver Cromwell's Parliament ruled until 1660, when the monarchy was restored with Charles II returning from exile. The dashing young king landed in Dover where he spent the night in a mansion now known as the Restoration House.

Statue of Sir Winston Churchill on the village green at Westerham by Oscar Nemon (1906–85), which stands on a base of Yugoslavian stone, the gift of Marshal Tito. iStock

Conflicts with France and the Netherlands dominated the 17th century and Kent became crucial in the nation's maritime defence with increased fortification along the Medway. A great many warships were built at Chatham including, Nelson's HMS Victory, launched in 1765. The remains of some warships can be seen at the Chatham Dockyard museum today.

THE NAPOLEONIC WARS: TUNNELS, TOWERS AND SMUGGLERS

The war with post-revolutionary France between 1805 and 1815 saw Dover become a garrison town with 2,000 men stationed in secret tunnels beneath the castle. Over a hundred Martello towers were built for artillery along the Kent coast and they survive

Martello Tower at Folkestone iStock

at Dover, Hythe, Sandgate and other locations, many now converted into private homes. English Heritage has restored the Dymchurch Martello Tower.

Smuggling, or 'owling', as this nocturnal activity was known, began in the 14th century along the coast and on the misty marshes of Romney with wool going across the Channel to Holland and Belgium.

The trade became more and more lucrative with Dutch gin and tobacco, French brandy and lace being smuggled into England. Many towns in Kent from Ramsgate to Rochester prospered as a result and smugglers like Samuel Jackson (aka Slippery Sam) from Canterbury, executed in 1760, became notorious.

By the 19th century, the war with France and heavy import duties increased the demand for luxury goods and organised gangs warred with the 'Revenue Men'. Dymchurch became infamous and today celebrates its smuggling history with an annual festival dedicated to Doctor Syn, the vicar-by-day-smuggler-by-night hero created by Russell Thorndike in his novels.

Five and twenty ponies,

Trotting through the dark –

Brandy for the Parson,

'Baccy for the Clerk.

Laces for a lady; letters for a spy,

Watch the wall my darling while

the Gentlemen go by!

'The Smugglers' Song'
by RUDYARD KIPLING (1911)

THE INDUSTRIAL REVOLUTION: DOCKS AND MINES

In the 19th and early 20th centuries, paper mills, tanneries and the clothing industry flourished in the Medway towns and shipbuilding grew at Chatham. During World War II, 1360 ships including HMS Ajax were refitted in Chatham Dockyards.

In 1890 coal was discovered at Shakespeare Cliff during the very first Channel Tunnel excavations and dozens of collieries sprang up, served by the East Kent Light Railway. Tilmanstone and Betteshanger were the last mines to close in 1986 and 1989.

ROYAL TUNBRIDGE WELLS: SHOPPING AND SPAS

In 1835 Princess Victoria visited Tunbridge Wells and frequently returned as queen with her husband Albert. The royal visits made this spa resort, with its 17th-century covered

The HMS Gannet, at the former Royal Naval dockyard at Chatham, was built in 1878 and powered by both steam and sail. iStock

Shopping in the Pantiles, Royal Tunbridge Wells iStock

shopping area, The Pantiles, as popular as it had been during the days of Beau Nash and the Regency.

The town acquired gas lighting, an omnibus service and a railway station so the prosperous middle classes flocked from London, many choosing to build houses there. The Opera House opened in 1902 and the town received its 'Royal' prefix from Edward VII in 1909. *'Disgusted of Tunbridge Wells'* has become a humorous byword for conservative Middle England.

THE GARDEN OF ENGLAND: ORCHARDS, OAST HOUSES AND HOP-PICKING

With its fertile soil and warm climate, farming flourished in Kent for centuries giving the county a reputation as 'The Garden of England'. Kent's sheep grazing at Romney Marshes, orchards of apples, pears and cherries, and fields of wheat, oilseed rape and vegetables kept the capital supplied with food and beverages. Itinerant Romany gypsies and travellers from Ireland provided the labour for soft fruit and potato picking. Hops, first introduced in the 16th century, required an army of pickers – by 1724 there were 6,000 acres of hop gardens in East Kent alone. In the 19th and 20th centuries, poor Londoners, from the East End

Oast House iStock

and south-east London districts like Deptford, were arriving by train to pick hops. They treated this seasonal work as a welcome country holiday. Small breweries, cider-pressers and barrel makers (coopers) abounded in the towns and villages. Unique pointed oast houses for drying hops still dot the countryside; there is a working oast house museum at Sandling. Hop-picking died out as a seasonal job with mechanisation in the 1950s but Kent still employs more people in agriculture than any other county.

Hops blossom in 'The Garden of England' iStock

Hop-pickers gather round the camp fire in Yalding 1944
Creative Commons

Ah me, how pleasant to go down
From the forlorn and faded town
To Kentish wood and fold and lane,
And breathe God's blessed air again;
Where glorious yellow corn-fields blaze
And nuts hang over woodland ways.
To pick the sweet keen-scented hops,
(See from each pole a dream-wreath drops)
To toil all day in pure clear air,
Laughter and sunshine everywhere –
With reddening woods and sweet wet soil
And well-earned rest and honest toil.

From 'Hop Picking'
by EDITH NESBIT (1888)

Famous Locals Past and Present

Science fiction writer **Herbert George Wells** was born to a shopkeeper-cum-Kent county cricketer and his wife in Bromley in 1866. His first novel, *The Time Machine* (1895) was an instant success and he followed it with *The Island of Doctor Moreau* (1896), *The Invisible Man* (1897) and *The War of the Worlds* (1898) – a radio adaptation, with Orson Welles announcing an alien invasion, caused panic in America when it was broadcast in 1938. He foresaw the splitting of the atom and the creation of atomic bombs in *The World Set Free* (1914). His 1916 comedy of English village

Writer H.G. Wells Creative Commons

life *Mr Britling Sees It Through* was very popular. A socialist, Wells laid out his views on human progress in *The Outline of History* (1920). He died in 1946.

Sir Edward Heath, Conservative prime minister from 1970 to 1974, was born in Broadstairs in 1916 and educated at Chatham House Grammar in Ramsgate then at Balliol College, Oxford where he won the college's organ scholarship. He served in the Royal Artillery during World War II then joined the Civil Service. He became Member of Parliament for Bexley in 1950. His most significant political achievement was taking Britain into the European Union. Ousted as Conservative leader by Margaret Thatcher, he remained in the Commons as an outspoken backbencher and, from 1992, as 'Father of the House', the oldest MP, until he retired in 2001. As well as being a skilled politician, he was an author, musician, and a prize-winning yachtsman. He died in 2005 aged 89.

Sir Mick Jagger, songwriter and rock star, was born in Dartford in 1943 and went to Dartford Grammar School where he met Keith Richards and discovered a mutual love of rock 'n' roll musicians like Little Richard. Mick went to The London School of Economics and formed the Rolling Stones (named after a Muddy Waters tune) with Brian Jones and Keith Richards, doing their first gig at The

Mick Jagger, pictured left, enjoys worldwide fame. The Republic of Congo even issued this Rolling Stones postage stamp in 2009. iStock

Marquee Club in 1962. '(I Can't Get No) Satisfaction', recorded with new band members Bill Wyman and Charlie Watts, became the Stones' first international hit in 1965. Fame, controversy and huge hits like Exile on Main Street (1972) followed. Jagger starred in the 1970 movies Performance and Ned Kelly. In 2002 he was knighted. The Stones still tour to sold-out venues.

Tracey Emin CBE was born in 1963 to a British Romany mother and a Turkish-Cypriot father who owned a hotel in Margate. Brought up in Margate, she graduated from Maidstone College of Art in 1986. She rose to fame as part of the Young British Artist (YBA) movement with controversial works such as Everyone I Have Ever Slept With 1963–1995 and the installation My Bed. She is now one of the first two female professors at The Royal Academy. In 2011 she was asked to open The Turner Contemporary Gallery in Margate. She has held exhibitions all over the world and was given the CBE for services to the arts in 2013. My Bed, owned by collector Charles Saatchi, sold for £2.2 million in 2014.

Dame Kelly Holmes OBE, athlete was born in Pembury in 1970, went to school in Tonbridge and joined Tonbridge Athletics Cub. At 18, she joined the Women's Royal Army Corps, later becoming a physical training instructor. Injury stopped her competing in the 1992 Olympic

Games but she became a full-time athlete in 1997 and gained a bronze in the 2000 Olympics. In the 2004 Athens Olympics, she broke the 1500 metres record, winning gold in this event and the 800 metres. She was BBC Sports Personality of the Year in 2004, before retiring the following year. She founded the DKH Legacy Trust to support young athletes and other young people in 2008.

Jack Dee at The British Comedy Awards 2007. Ron H Jones

Holmes at Athens 2004

Jack Dee, deadpan stand-up comedian, was born in Bromley in 1961 and grew up near Petts Wood. He worked as a waiter at The Ritz hotel and his first gig was after work at an open mic show at The Comedy Store in 1986. He started learning his craft on the comedy circuit and won the Perrier Best Newcomer Award at the Edinburgh Fringe Festival in 1991. Television shows followed including *Jack Dee's Saturday Night* and *Jack Dee's Happy Hour* in 1997, *Jack Dee Live at the Apollo* in 2004 and the BBC sitcom

Lead Balloon in 2007. He's a regular on BBC's *QI* and *Have I Got News For You* and took over the chair of BBC Radio 4's *I'm Sorry I Haven't A Clue* in 2009.

Orlando Bloom at the 2014 San Diego Comic Con International Gage Skidmore

Orlando Bloom, actor, was born in Canterbury in 1977. He made his film debut in *Wilde* (1997), opposite Stephen Fry, before entering the Guildhall School of Music and Drama in London. His big break was playing Legolas in *The Lord of the Rings* film trilogy (2001–3). He starred opposite Keira Knightley and Johnny Depp in *Pirates of the Caribbean: The Curse of the Black Pearl*, which was a blockbuster hit in 2003. He reprised his role as Will Turner in *Pirates of the Caribbean: Dead Man's Chest* (2006) and *Pirates of the Caribbean: At World's End* (2007). He sent himself up in a guest role in the sitcom *Extras* and has also appeared on the London stage and on Broadway as Romeo in *Romeo and Juliet* in 2013.

Singer Joss Stone was born in Dover in 1987 then brought up in Devon. The music of Dusty Springfield and Aretha Franklin inspired her to become a singer and, at just 14, she auditioned for a popular BBC show, *Star for a Night*. Her 2003 album *Soul Sessions* was highly acclaimed and in 2004 she was nominated for a MOBO Award and the Mercury Prize; in 2005

Joss Stone at Stockholm Jazz Festival 2009. Benoit Derrier

she won two Brit Awards. In 2006 she was the youngest woman to feature on The Times Rich List. Fame has its price and in 2011 police arrested two men near Stone's home for plotting to rob and murder her; they were found guilty at Exeter Crown Court in 2013.